Vocabulary *of* LIES

DIANN BANKS

Order this book online at www.trafford.com
or email orders@trafford.com

Most Trafford titles are also available at major online book retailers.

Printed in the United States of America.

ISBN: 978-1-4907-4063-8 (sc)
ISBN: 978-1-4907-4064-5 (hc)
ISBN: 978-1-4907-4065-2 (e)

Library of Congress Control Number: 2014911271

Trafford rev. 07/15/2014

 www.trafford.com
North America & international
toll-free: 1 888 232 4444 (USA & Canada)
fax: 812 355 4082

Contents

Preface vii

Acknowledgments ix

Introduction...xi

1. Not The Standard Dictionary Definition of a Lie 1

2. The Out-and-Out Lie (Unnecessary Lying) 9

3. The Abstract Lie 26

4. The Perfect Lie 31

5. Habitual Liars 35

6. Expert Liars..38

7. A Test For Perceived Liars (Check For Lies) 41

8. Livers of Lies 48

9. Putting Lies To Rest 52

10. Who Wants To Hear It...58

11. The Need To Lie 60

12. Ordinary Lies (Typical lies) 63

13. Why Lie?...76

14. Action Lies 81

15. What To Do...87

Summary 95

Appendix I: "Exclamations" 101

Appendix II: - Short Stories: 103

    Regina's Box 51

    Run Tell That 53

    Time Always Tells On Liars 66

    I Am Pretty And Smart 68

    Play Along Or Leave..................................74

    Is Lying the Better Policy? 79

    You Mean It 82

    Don't Leave Me Out...................................84

    Could Not Resist The Lie 92

Appendix III: Contributors............................... 105

Appendix IV: Photos and Tidbits 107

Preface

This easy to read book is insightful. It gives you an opportunity for self-examination. I enjoyed preparing the test. The case studies are all true but the names have been changed to protect me. Starting now, I will listen to and choose words that convey my message.

After reading this book you will be able to detect the unbalancing that is coupled with lying. You must clearly define and be aware of the relationships we develop, ensuring you receive what you expect. In all sincerity, you will certainly understand the importance of telling the truth.

Feedback. Interact. Tell your friends about "The Vocabulary of Lies." It is not an angry brow beating book rather one designed to reach others just from the advantage point of outcomes.

Plan to avoid the stumbling blocks that you read about in this book. Pick Temple's Giant Ranch Show that aired on television from 1952 to 1961. His motto was "Don't put off until tomorrow what you can do today!" Let's not deliberately manufacture a "lie"today that you will have to fix one tomorrow.

Proudly I salute myself for writing a much needed book to enlighten the minds of so many people who do not see the harm in telling a story. When I say story, that is just a nicety for the word "lie."

Imagination is a powerful tool. It is responsible for our creativity. Without it there would be no inventions or very much of anything productive and worthwhile in our society.

There would be no variety, no spice. In my journey of life I have experienced and participated in lying or lying situations. I find that the art of lying can be infectious.

While lies can be designed to harm us most times they simply are a means of protection for the liar. This book will dig deep into the many facets of lies and open up doors that lead to the core, the content, and the results of lying.

Acknowledgments

I am passionate about lying, I believe there must be others who share my passion. Balance in the universe rightly gives us lies and truth. At noontime, Toastmasters meeting, I gave a speech, "How These Great People Influenced My Life". After the speech several people asked if what I said was true. I told them yes, all I had said was true. Depending on the different people's opinion of my credibility and/or character determined whether they believed my speech to be true or false, a lie.

No excerpts of the speech but a list of those greats deceased and living follows: I am thankful to have met (deceased greats) Martin Luther King, Ralph Abernathy, Ozzie Davis, Patricia Harris, Dorothy Height, Steve McQueen, Nina Simone, Wilson Pickett, and Johnny Cochran. Also, I am thankful to have met (living greats) Muhammad Ali, Jesse Jackson, Sheila E, Regina Bell, Dee Dee Sharp, Patti Labelle, Patty Austin, Carol King, James Taylor, The Beatles, Paul McCarthy, James Ingrahm, Kareem Abdul Jabar, Herbie Hancock, and Chris Rock.

Thanks to their encouragement. I strive to be great.

Also, thank you Raymond for giving me the title for this, my first book. Moreover, thank you my beloved Mr. Banks for your support and confidence in me. Without you in my life, this book would never had been conceived or written.

This book came into fruition because of what would have been a lie if I had tried to finish any of my prior work before my birthday, June 28. It would not have happened because all the stories and poetry I wrote was no where near completion. As a child, my pen name was "Scratch.' I started this book fresh from scratch.

Introduction

If you are a believer of the Holy Bible, you may have read that a liar will not enter into the Kingdom of Heaven. There are over 100 scriptures about lies and liars. So, with that being said, what good is there in telling a lie? A good lie is clearly an oxymoron.

Consequences are not worth it, yet there is an art to lying. You will find that there are many ways to lie. In some cases you may not be aware of lying. Whether it is someone lying to or on you or if in fact you are doing the lying. When you are unknowingly doing the lying, it becomes second nature and your lying can very well become your truth.

Because you are clearly not aware or have not identified what you have done or said as a lie, you will continue lying.

In the long-run, you will discover that lies can cause you, as well as others, pain. The intentions behind a lie are always pertinent. If your lie serves to protect someone's feelings or protect you from some harm or injury, you may find it useful in the end or it may pop up later to bite.

This book will help you identify lies. Both lies that you tell or that are told to you will be listed and demonstrated in scenarios, case studies, and short stories The lies we entertain are pointed toward others, the lies they tell. We recognize others' actions as well as what they say. It is so much easier to accuse another person of lying rather than to objectively see your own actions.

Once you have completed this book, the impact of lies in your life will diminish. It will not matter which side of the lie you are on, your experience will be more enlightening than threatening. Preparation always takes the sting out of surprise. In other words, do not be surprised that you very well may witness a lie, be lied on, or tell a lie yourself.

Many times we sincerely do not have a clue as to if a person is being truthful or for that matter how much of the truth we know and tell. Most times people ask questions anticipating the answers. When the answer is not the desired answer, is the answer a lie? How do we label lies? What good or damage can a perceived lie affect your everyday life?

1. Not The Standard Dictionary Definition of a Lie

Before I give you my definitions of "lie." I will give you the computer's dictionary definition of vocabulary. I chose – the system of techniques or symbols serving as a means of expression (as in arts or crafts) as my first and, a listing of the words used in some enterprises as my second.

When a person lies, it is a meaningful expression. There is an art to lying and most times, the liar is crafty. Vocabulary becomes more than just a listing of words. Usage plays a crucial part. Therefore in discussing the why, how, what, when, and where of lies, I had to share the role vocabulary plays in lies.

People lie for a number of reasons with as many terms to stand in for the term lie. They are restructuring, exaggeration, minimization, denial, sarcasm, and fabrication. All these plus more compose the vocabulary of lies. It is funny that the same vocabulary you use to tell the truth you can use to tell a lie.

This is not how any dictionary that you will read defines a lie. A lie is something that is said or done that the recipient does not want to believe as being true. It does not matter how much credence, proof, or explanations.....pleas, crying, or swears occur. The recipient has a made up mind to believe or disbelieve some or none of what is experienced.

In other words, while something can be absolutely true. Whether that is the case or not depends on the person's judgment and conclusion. A person's disbelief of the truth is determined a lie. "I just don't believe it" boils down to a lie for that person. It is always a judgment call.

I have found a lie to be a person blatantly telling you that they do not like the way you treat them or talk to them, but the person continues to call you and persists to be in your company. Now whether the person is lying to you or if they are lying to themselves becomes the issue. Likewise, at times people can be overheard saying that they will try anything and once approached with a question of "Have you tried....?" Surprisingly, the person will readily respond, "No. I have not." Do you wonder why they will continue to believe that the first statement that they made is not now untrue. The person will challenge you should you say, "Well then. You have not tried everything."

Again, the person will insist, "Yes. Everything but that." Without any hesitation, without ever entertaining the thought that what they are saying is in fact not true, but a lie. As innocent as this can be, a lie is just that a lie. Although harmless, identifiably not the same as the truth. A simple example, yet, one that will make the point of the argument that could be just the technicality that renders the shadow of a doubt should a question be asked in a courtroom. This often times is just the shadow of a doubt that can lead to a person's innocence or guilt.

Most times when people see things that are beyond their belief or hear things that they perceive as impossible, they chalk it up as a lie. You can hear it in their responses. "Yea, right." "Sure you're right." "Oh, I'm Susie Sausage Head." Often times, these responses will shut a person down. The person will not continue to explain because of the offense that has been taken to those responses.

There are instances when people have been observed exhausted and outdone trying to ensure that someone believes what they are saying. Their minds are completely blown recalling the effort that was put forth in their explanations and the discontent expressed to them coupled with being told "that's a lie." It is customary to hear in a conversation centered around this type of discord "prove it."

While some things can be proven many things cannot. The person or people have to make a decision to accept the statement as true or decline the statement as false. We are always in some respect being faced with the choice of true or false. It begins early in our lives with true or false tests. True or false tests many times are the preferred tests because they are considered easy. But are they really.

Time after time I can remember taking a true and false test and knowing that a question was true later to find that it was clearly false. That happens mainly because of how the question is framed. Also, we can select the wrong answer if we do not carefully read the question.

Listening is not unlike reading. Should the question be posed to us orally, we must be careful, attentive listeners. One word can make a true statement false and vice versa. Either a statement is correct or incorrect, true or false.

Mind sets are responsible for so many things that are considered lies. People who have been raised to believe superstitions for example will not accept the real facts only what they are accustomed to believing which makes those other things "lies." In most cases, words like falsehoods and untruths have been used instead of the term "lies." There is much usage of the words "fibs"and "fabrications" instead of using the term "lies."

Many times when people do not want to face the pain of a situation, they will call something a lie. So in reality, lies are widespread and most times unintentional and innocent.

Nonetheless, lies are detrimental and can lead people off track, in the wrong direction, and missing out completely.

Questions are asked where people know the answer but they want confirmation by asking the question anyway. Usually when people ask questions that relate to emotions, such as "Do you love me?" The reply of "Yes" is the anticipated. If the respondent wants to say "No" but in order not to put the relationship at risk or hurt the person's feelings, the response will be "Yes." The lie is the redeeming factor at the time, while in the near future a series of lies will follow because there certainly will be other questions that will be in line with that first question.

However we categorize and/or label a lie, chances are that eventually the truth will come out. Postponing the truth can be more upsetting to the situation than initially telling the truth from the start.

Without a question being asked, conclusions can be drawn from how one perceives a potential response. Instances present themselves where one will anticipate a response based on past experiences with that person or with another person. Either way, when a person operates based on a perceived answer it possibly could be a lie.

In reality, the person is guessing and behaving as if he/she knows. At times should the person expect a negative response and receives a positive response, it is a good thing. But in cases where the person anticipates a positive response and gets a negative response, the person can go into a denial zone and reject the answer which will make matters worse or they can be devastated by the answer and continue to cling to the perceived lie that he/she has manufactured.

People can lie to you and you can lie to yourself. Neither is a good or healthy state because it will not add up later. Surely, it is better to be truthful with yourself. When you are not sure about something and you need an answer, do not convince yourself that you have the answer just ask the question. Be brave enough to accept it regardless if it is one that you want to hear or not. It is far better to be on track so that you can move forward with your life.

Linda always wanted to hear good things about herself and her situations. She would tell you about an incident and express how she felt about it expecting the response to line up with hers. Consequently, as the responses differed, she would simply say "just tell me what I want to hear." For example, she asked her boyfriend of 2 months if he loved her and before he could answer, she said, "Lie to me."

There are many types of lies and liars that I have just selected those that, in my opinion, top the list. The following chapters will discuss them and hopefully, you will be able to identify with them and if not, you will learn how to recognize them in the future. After all the various types of lies have been told, we need to know how to deal with them.

First and foremost, we need to forgive. Of course, there will be times when you feel that it is just an unforgivable situation, but we must look at ourselves and be considerate. Sometimes we need to forgive ourselves. When we are sworn to secrecy and/or told things in confidence and then we are asked for the information, we can choose to tell it, lie, or simply say "I know, but I cannot tell you." The best response is always going to be the one that we can live with.

My take on that is simply—I have met this woman's six year old grand daughter and she is absolutely gorgeous. I am sure Grace, like her grandmother, has passed on the same words of wisdom to her.

We have been told that beauty is in the eye of the beholder and that is as close to the truth as anything. As we grow and mature, we must be proactive and not allow any insecurities, low-esteem, or false prides to direct our relationships with others. People treat us the way we allow them to treat us. When we send out vibrations of "I'm better, prettier, and smarter", most times people are thinking "than who." I certainly thought it when I heard it. Clearly, it was true for Grace but it was a solid lie to me.

I believe people treat Grace badly because of her condescending, know-it-all, I'm better than you attitude.

Never could I put my finger on why Grace behaved so rudely. That conversation answered my question. The impact of it was forceful enough to make this book. Hopefully, you do not share any similar views such as Grace.

2. The Out-and-Out Lie
(Unnecessary Lying)

This type of lie is the one that everybody tags. Make no mistake about it. It sounds like a lie and it was unnecessary. Most times with the out-and-out lie, the person gets called on it. "You're lying." Of course, the liar does not admit to the lie. I will present the same scenario three times throughout this book. We will identify the dialogue as speaker #1-3 and liar #1-3.

First Scenario: The out-and-out lie

Speaker #1:   Where are you going?
Liar #1:   To the store?
Two hours later:
Speaker #1:   What did you get from the store?
Liar #1:   What?

This out-and-out liar forgot the lie. This scenario will be repeated with other liars later in the book. All in all, they all are lying. Some just better than others. Some a lot more believable than the out-and-out liar.

The out-and-out lie is not hard to identify. I am sure that you can give many examples of preposterous things that people say that as they are saying them you know it is a lie. First, it is so far fetched that there is no way that it could be true and it sounds like a lie.

Another determining factor of a lie is the look on the person's face. Signs of discomfort and even perspiration also will indicate that the person is telling a laugh. In some cases, when a person cannot keep a straight face or keep the lie going, the person may break out in laughter or in extreme cases, confess–change the lie—tell the truth.

Out-and-out lies are the most hurtful. They can also masquerade through omission. When you are not told something that is relevant, and later you find out, the out-and-out liar will always respond in these ways:

1) I did tell you. You must have forgotten.
2) You did not ask me.
3) I thought you knew.
4) Why would I tell you something like that.

5) I didn't think you wanted to know.
6) You knew.

Sometimes it is better that your thoughts on a particular subject be left unsaid. When putting your thoughts into words it is always only what a person is willing to reveal. It can be difficult pulling your thoughts together when you know that you have to be guarded from one reason or another. You must be careful that whatever you do so say, that you do not lie.

These types of liars always escalate the situation with more lies. Simple questions such as: "What fragrance are you wearing?" generates the direct answer, Chanel, Beyonce, Cher. But most often, the responses could range from "I don't know what I put on this morning" to "I have a number of fragrances and lotions, I don't know what you are smelling."

While these could all be true statements they tend to sound like a lie. Sincerity trumps most answers. A person who is doing the best to give a truthful answer holds more credibility even if what they are saying is a total lie. For instance, a person can give inaccurate information because the information was given to them. That person embraced that information as truth and passed it on as truth. This is not a cultivated lie rather information received from what was considered a reliable source.

Misleading information such as the wrong directions could be by design or accident. Many people will tell you they know how to get somewhere and give you the wrong directions with all surety that they know what they are talking about. Can we classify an occurrence of this sort as a lie? Of course, it depends on the receiver. Many people buffer what they are told. They take the high road and give the person the benefit of the doubt. Should they be mislead or actually lied to, you will find these people saying "they didn't mean it" or "they were doing the best that they knew how". Again, who is to say either way.

Case Study:

"How old is your daughter?" asked the passenger sitting beside me on the bus. Well, Maria thought. Does she see my daughter? Am I even talking to her, I'm on my cell phone. Maria hesitates, she is thinking...I should say none of your business but finally Maria answers the passenger saying "Twenty-two."

To completely understand this case study you would have had to have more information to know that the answer was a ridiculous lie. Maria was a teenager.

Case Study:

Henry promised to purchase a set of earphones for his son, Tim. Henry told Tim that he would meet him at his school at the close of the school day. Tim waited for two hours with no signs of Henry. While Tim was waiting his emotions went from excitement, to impatience, to anxiety, to frustration, to anger. Disappointed that Henry did not show up he ran the entire block home. When he approached his house, Henry was sitting on the front porch. Although Tim was perplexed, the emotions inside of him instantly changed from anger to joy.

Before Tim could say a word, Henry yelled out "Where have you been? I have been waiting for you for two hours." Tim discerned from Henry's tone that he was angry. Tim replied, "I was waiting for you for two hours outside of my school." Henry in an angrier voice yelled, "I told you I would meet you at your house not your school." Tim a little disgusted thought, the nerve of him. He clearly told me to meet him at the school at the closing of class.

At this point, Tim's excitement overwhelmed his disbelief and he accepted the lie. His goal was simply to receive the earphones. So it seemed, in an instant, Tim began to jump up and down and asked Henry to forgive hm. Tim said he was sorry that he misunderstood where he should have been. Henry's anger was now transformed into guilt. He told Tim that he was sorry and maybe he was the one who got it wrong. They exchanged hugs and Henry gave Tim the earphones.

Had Henry told an out-and-out lie? Or could he gotten his wires crossed? This was not Tim's concern. Tim told a lie to keep the peace and get his earphones. Before Henry left, he apologized again to Tim and stated that in the future they would confirm their meeting place to be sure that they both were on the same page. This situation was handled well. Easily, this could have gone another way. Tim was in his right to tell Henry that he was lying. They had agreed upon meeting at the school. The end result may have been no earphones for Tim. This was a wise decision that Tim made at 13 years old. He is well on his way towards not labeling people as liars and taking the high road even though his feelings were hurt and he was angry he did not allow himself to be a victim rather a victor.

When you are confronted with a lie, it is not always wise to address it. You must weigh the situation and give the person the benefit of the doubt. Good advice to follow is to look before you leap and think before you speak.

On occasion, you or the other person may get mixed up or completely forget. There will be times when you may have an appointment with someone and you double book. You are at a movie or in a restaurant and realize that someone is waiting for you.

Doing the responsible thing of calling and saying "I forgot, etc." is the appropriate thing to do. Face it. Do not wait until you are called on it and then say, "I thought we were supposed to meet some other time" which you know to be a lie. Lies are contagious. Should you get into the habit of lying to cover up your mistakes you are setting a trap for yourself down the line.

Branding a person as a liar is a harsh, crucial, dangerous, and sometimes unfair labeling. On the other hand, it can be helpful because it serves as a warning to be on guard. Once a person is labeled as a liar, you tend to expect a lie from them in the course of any conversation. In passing on information that you received from such a person you can almost always get a reaction of "She told you that!

A valuable lesson that can be learned from passing on information that you are not vested in should be not to gossip. When it isn't the truth it puts your reputation in jeopardy.

You should have known better than to believe that coming from her." You may not have been aware of this woman's reputation as a liar and now you look at her in another light and are cautious in what you believe of what she says as well as what you say to her. As you know, what you say to a person can also be twisted thus putting you in a similar light. Now, people can be somewhere corrupting your reputation.

Out-and out lies come to light. Lying about your skill level is discovered when you take on an assignment that you cannot complete successfully. Unacceptable performance is an embarrassment for you as well as the person who is depending on the accuracy.

While many people lie about their education level, experience, and skill level to obtain status, acceptance, and positions, that feeling of inadequacy is tearing them apart. In these cases, the solution is go out and get the training you need to do what you want to do and be who you profess.

This is much like identity theft, which, by the way is also a lie. When you present yourself as someone who you are not, how long can you keep up the act. In the movie, "What's Love Got to Do With It?" Angela Bassett was playing the role of Tina Turner. There was a scene where she says to

Laurence Fishborne, who was playing the part of Ike Turner "I was wondering when the real Ike Turner was going to show up."

Fraud is another out-and-out lie. Categories of fraud are numerous. When a person behaves unlike who they are, that is fraudulent behavior. Identity theft is fraud. Writing a check for $10 dollars on a zero account balance is fraud. These may be small acts of fraud yet fraud nonetheless. There is a practice of fraud that occurs too often in a day on the internet and that is when users paint false pictures of themselves with embellished information.

Shopping signs most often promote lies as well as the layout of products in the store. How many times have you seen advertisements for one brand and once you get into the store that brand is not available but there is another brand placed under the advertisement that caused you to come into the store in the first place? Or the sale price is for the 8 oz bottle but there are no 8 oz bottles rather 10 oz bottles. Lies, all lies. The proper term for this is bait and switch. It is a lie.

Nobody is asking the liar anything. Out of the blue, the liar just begins telling you "tales"–"stories"–"LIES." The liar does this in hopes of painting a picture of himself/herself that glorifies. Obviously, this type of lying is done to mislead the other person. Most times with adults, these liars are con artists and swindlers. They have an ulterior motive—to get over on you. This person can associate, know, or be related to successful or well-to-do people and want to impress you that they are as well. They can flash money that they don't have in hopes of getting large sums of money from you in the near future. I am sure you have heard of these types of scams and hopefully, you have not been a victim of any.

Now, there are exceptions to every situation. If this person has low self-esteem, it could be that building up the image will make him/her feel better about himself/herself and he/she may even develop into this person they want you to believe them to be.

Be honest. If you are applying for a loan at a bank and you adjust some things and omit others in an effort to get financial assistance, you will be found out. Then, the financial institution will not be able to trust you enough to grant you a loan. You cannot stretch facts.

Why people lie about hard facts that can be researched, investigated, and checked out is mind boggling. I have found that people will work with you when they know who you are and can depend on you for being honest.

First impressions are always thought of as lasting ones. We are told to make a good first impression. To successfully do this we must have a good sense of who we are and present ourselves honestly.

This lesson was one I learned on the job. I had interviewed for a receptionist position. Qualifying factors for this position included: a neat appearance, a pleasant attitude, and articulate language, among other things. What you see is what you get. The interviewer saw all the qualities he sought for this receptionist position. I was hired.

One week passed and the interviewer saw me at my desk and said. If you had come to the interview the way you are looking today, I would not have hired you. Clearly,

I understood what he meant. Confidence of having the job superseded my judgment. I had to maintain that image. While my attitude was consistently pleasant and there was no problem with my articulation. My hair was different (a different length and color–a wig) and my dress was a little too casual unlike the suit that I wore to the interview. I had passed myself off as a professional looking receptionist and I realized that I had to revert back to that image to retain my job. It was not me. I loved change. Job search. I had to find a job that was a good fit for me–one that I would not have to work at before I began work. At my next interview, I openly asked what was expected of me and clearly stated what I would bring to the table.

This interviewer and I were then on the same page and neither of us foresaw any surprises.

Another example of an action lie is, seeing a person in a military uniform you would assume that the person was a soldier. Or if a person was dressed like a fireman-mailman-police officer-physician you would believe what you saw. Nonetheless, these people could be projecting a false image and up to no good. We see in our everyday lives how people use uniforms and titles to convince others that they are reputable and then rob or kill them.

My pet peeve of an action lie is person professing to be a certain kind of person and showing something different.

That is when a person is so sweet and holy to some and mean and unholy to others. Consistency whatever is displayed is the direction of right. A person's actions can or cannot tell you who they are. Excuses such as, "I'm having a bad day" or "You caught me at the wrong time" does not change a person's character. Acting out of character is a lie.

Children also do a lot of unnecessary lying. Their motivation is escaping the world that they are in and going to a more comfortable place. For example, a child may share a bed with several other siblings and the child's friend may have their own room.

The child uses his/her imagination and describes the room to the friend and elaborates to outdo and outshine the friend. While as a child, this can be harmless it could also turn for the worse should the child find a comfort zone and a way out of other situations.

In some cases, when a child is believed and feels that "I'm good at this," this can become a habit and is attached to most every situation the child encounters on into adulthood. When children are found out as lying, correction should take place. They need to know how detrimental lying is and the cause and effects of it. The child needs to be able to make a decision as to what he/she will choose.

Case Study:

Skipping an afternoon art class sounded like a great idea to Sandra, Glenda, JoAnna, and Louise. Sandra knew just the perfect place to go to hook school. All the girls agree they would go to Sandra's cousin's house and play card games. This was the first time that any of these girls had cut class. When the clock approached three o'clock. The girls left Sandra's cousin's house and suddenly realized they had to have a story to tell their teachers the next day. They got a story together, rehearsed it over and over and then left to go to their perspective homes.

The next day all the girls were called into the principal's office. When Louise reached the office, the other girls were leaving. They did not give her any eye contact and she did not know what to expect. Louise told her story to the principal and he kept saying, "Tell the truth". Louise stuck to her story because the girls had decided yesterday that they would stick to their story no matter what. After five minutes had passed, the principal gave up and told Louise that everyone had told the truth about the card game. Louise was the only girl punished for playing hooky from art class. Her punishment was harsh. She was put into a social adjustment class with slow, misbehaving students for one week. The other girls were ashamed that they had told the truth but in fact lied to Louise. Louise was ashamed that she had kept her word with the girls and lied to the principal.

The principal taught Louise the lesson that she could not win with a lie. Although all of the girls committed the same offense, they did not handle the situation the same. Louise thought it must be a crime to lie because crime does not pay, then lies do not pay either.

Scenario 2: Unnecessary Lying

Liar #2:	Hey, I am going to the store.
Speaker #2:	Okay.
Two hours later:	
Speaker #2:	What did you get from the store?
Liar #2:	I didn't go to the store.
Speaker #2:	You said you were going to the store.
Liar #2:	I never said I was going to the store.
Speaker #2:	Yes you did. You said you were going to the store.
Liar #2:	I don't know what you are talking about.

Now the speaker in this case knows that this direction of the conversation is going to continue because in past situations a straight answer was impossible. The speaker dare not ask this unnecessary liar where he/she was for two hours because the response will be mind boggling. Then again, the liar may tell another lie or stick to the lie.

Guessing and making up lies seems to be a waste of energy. But people do it without thinking about the consequences. They are covering something that will make them uncomfortable should they tell the truth. Unnecessary lying? No. Not for the liar. Another example of a lie that may seem unnecessary to one can be quite necessary to another.

Carolyn was dating a young man, Troy. Carolyn and Troy fussed and fought all the time. Carolyn desperately wanted to get out of the relationship but Troy threatened to kill her if she left him. In the meantime, Carolyn got pregnant. She did not tell anyone. Before it was evident that she was pregnant Troy was arrested for burglary and was sent to prison.

When Troy returned home from prison, some five years later, his neighborhood crew told him Carolyn had a baby boy and he looked just like him. Troy raced to Carolyn's house and was greeted by Carolyn's mother, Rose. Rose told him "It does not matter what you heard, that baby is not yours."

To make a long story short, now the baby is a teenager and everyone in the neighborhood told him about how bad his father was when he was a teenager and how he looked just like Troy. Carolyn's teenage son replied "Oh, he's not my father." and continued on his way.

Should Carolyn's son need an organ that Troy could and would be more than willing to donate, it would not happen because while Troy always held on to the fact that Carolyn's son was his son, Carolyn continued to deny it. Thinking positively, this lie worked out for Carolyn in several ways: 1) She was free of Troy, 2) Her son could be free of Troy's influence, and 3) Why did her son have to know the truth, he did not need Troy for anything at present.

Carolyn clearly viewed this as a necessary lie. What about you? Would you have looked up the road–towards the future if you were in that situation or would you have lied as Carolyn did?

Changes to one's appearance can be considered lies if asked and you do not tell the truth or if you are not asked and you are simply portraying something as being the truth that is a lie. These can be as simple as a nose job, lip implants, contacts, eyelash extensions, acrylic nails, hair extensions, wigs, breast implants,—I could go on and on.

There have been numerous arguments and break-ups surrounding someone lying about some aspect of their appearance being modified. Most men have expressed the fact that they prefer natural beauty. Sadly enough, they cannot recognize it and only when they stumble over the truth can they face how they really feel about their belief.

In other words, "fake". I was in a relationship when I met a man when my hair was braided. To my surprise he feel in love with my braids and not me. One day I told him I was going to the hairdressers and he put a huge smile on his face. Little did I know he was expecting to see this long flowing hair because I was taking my braids out–little did he know that I was getting my hair cut into a Hale Berry style.

Once I met him for dinner, his demeanor was different. He was distant and cold. I asked him what was wrong and he asked me why did I cut my hair. Unbelievable. It seemed obvious to me that he knew my braids were extensions, but they were human hair and he was fooled although that was not my intention. He told me I was fake and that I had led him to believe that the braids were my hair. Yes. He expressed his feelings of discontent and betrayal. It was hilarious to me but he was devastated and never treated me the same after that day.

3. The Abstract Lie

An abstract lie can be described as a lie that depending on what side of the lie you are on may not be detected. There are numerous categories within the abstract lie. I will illustrate a variety of them starting with half trues, omissions, and vagueness.

Many of us lie without thinking about it as lying. How many times have you let the phone ring because you did not want to take the call? The person on the other end believes you are not available to take the call while in reality you are available but won't take the call. Your answering machine will say you are not at home—you are; or you are not available–you are.

Actually, your actions are creating the lie. Half trues can also fall in the category of abstract lies.

Case Study:

Ralph had a glass eye. He was scheduled to get an operation to receive a real eye. I visited him in the hospital an hour before it was time for the operation. On my way home, as I looked out of the window on the bus, I could not believe my eyes. I saw Ralph, standing on the corner. Was my eyes playing tricks on me? A few minutes ago, I left him in his hospital bed having been prepped for an eye operation. There he was with the bandage still on his eye. Hastily, I rang the bell and jumped off the bus to approach Ralph.

Ralph stopped me in my tracks as his body language said "wait, I'm busy." A man was standing there talking to Ralph and giving him money. I overheard the man say "I hope this will help you get your eye. Ralph had told this man that he was put out of the hospital because he did not have the money to get a new eye. A lie. The truth was, Ralph was afraid to get the operation and slipped out of the hospital.

It only took one man to inquire about his eye for him to take advantage of the opportunity to lie and get money at the same time. He took this sympathy act on the road. So without saying a word, Ralph presented a visual lie and then followed it up with a verbal lie. Striking while the iron was hot is exactly what Ralph did. He used a half-truth and adjusted it to his advantage to pass it on as the whole truth. By the way, need I remind you that a half-truth is a lie. Doctors have diagnosed health problems for individuals and the individuals inadvertently reject the prognosis.

In one case, a doctor explained to a patient that if he should take another drink that he would die. The patient had a "sure you right" moment and continued to drink. On the patient's next visit to the doctor, the doctor told him if you continue to drink, you will be dead in five years. We know the patient continued to drink. He did not believe the doctor knew what he was talking about.

Five years later the patient was in the hospital suffering from a brain tumor. The patient insisted that the condition had nothing to do with the fact that he continued to drink. This is another example of an abstract lie. One more drink translated into, "in the near future." In this case, five years.

Omission, as well as vagueness, are types of abstract lies. When a person assumes something about you that is not true and you do not correct them, you are perpetrating a lie.

Responses such as "you never asked me", "I thought you knew", and "didn't I tell you", are a few defenses used to address the accusations of lying. Omissions always are the most difficult lies to get a person to admit. Because, nothing was said.

Telling the truth is a means of coming to terms with oneself and the world.. There is no better way to keep down confusion and conflict than to be truthful. Certainly everyone will not be prepared to accept the truth or your truth because most times people can receive information better from people they like and/or know as opposed to people they particularly do not trust, like or respect their opinion.

For example, my mother gets excellent suggestions and advice from her friends that I endorse. But only should her doctor tell her the very same thing that we have told her for years, does she hear, and for the first time.

My mother buys in and does what she could have done years ago. I am reminded when I have been the bearer of bad news to a group of people. My supervisor would echo, "They will take it better if it comes from you." I am sure you have heard, don't kill the messenger. It means you had absolutely nothing to do with the bad or unpleasant message.

Formulated opinions of others can divide and sometimes destroy relationships. What you see is not always what you get. Another adage "you can't judge the book by its cover" supports this next partial case study:

Case study:

Jane was sitting in the front of her shorthand class opening and then reading a letter "I'm going to medical school to become a doctor." All of a sudden, laughter broke out from the back of the room. Please, you, a doctor? You ain't gonna be anybody."

We don't know why Jane received this negative outbreak from one of her classmates. However, her letter was her proof but the impression she had made on someone was not in sync with her good news. Without that letter, if challenged, the entire class would have considered what Jane said to be a lie.

It is evident that when proof is provided to support a statement, that statement becomes more believable. For example, if a person says, "I graduated from Brown University in 1971" then they give you the yearbook with their picture in it, I'm certain that you are convinced. This seems true but in fact can be a lie. From personal experience, my graduation picture was in the yearbook but I did not do my student teaching that semester, a requirement for graduation.

Now certain official documents are what they are. For example, your birth certificate, social security card, driver's license, diploma, and marriage license are not as questionable as other pieces of proof.

4. The Perfect Lie

What an oxymoron! What do you think a perfect lie sounds like or looks like? Give up? The truth!!! There is no such thing as a perfect lie or is there. The thing about what liars consider a perfect lie is - anything the liar says or does intentionally and is not called on.

It can be called "pulling the wool over them", "getting away with murder",

Some people look at another way of not being caught in a lie is to tell a lie that includes someone who will not be available for consultation. For example, people who do not speak to each other, people who are unattainable in other places to include dead. People will tell lies on the dead knowing that there is no way to be refuted.

Scenario 3: The Perfect Lie

Speaker #3:   Where are you going?
Liar #3:   To the store?

Two hours later:

Speaker #3:   What did you get from the store?

Liar #3   goes into his/her pocket and pulls out a
                 notepad that he/she already had.

Liar #3:   This notepad. I had to go to four
                 drugstores before I could find it. You
                 know these are the ones I have to have
                 for my job. I saw Sylvia, John Counts
                 daughter, in the store. She told me to
                 tell you hello.

While this sounds good to the liar, the speaker knows
better. First and foremost, the notebook is not in a bag and
if it was so hard to find and so imperative to the liar's job,
certainly the purchase would have exceeded (1) one.

Moreover, speaker #3 has no way to contact Sylvia who
she met once, at a funeral, John Counts. "I forgot." Really. In
many cases, there are occurrences when one forgets while in
other instances it is a cope out. Yes, "I forgot" can pass as a
perfect lie. Especially when certain factors are present, such as
illness and/or age, "I forgot" can be believed.

Dementia, alzheimers', amnesia, schizophrenia all
legitimate causes of forgetfulness. In the case of the first two
(dementia and alzheimers) the person is not always truthful

about forgetting. Since they already have an excuse, they use it.

Ruth's 83 year-old mother has dementia. She remembers vividly the things that occurred in her youth and cannot remember something that she was talking about just a few minutes passed. Ruth's daughter, Barbara impresses upon her mother that she has to drink at least two bottles of water daily. When Barbara visits Ruth to replenish her water supply, she finds that after a week 20 bottles of water remain instead of 10. "Mom, you haven't been drinking your water" said Ruth. "Yes I have. But sometimes, I forget." "Did you forget to take your medicine?" asked Barbara as she checks the medicine she finds that Ruth in fact had diligently taken her blood pressure medicine. "No, I take my medicine with a very little water, I don't like water." explained Ruth.

Ruth did not forget to drink two bottles of water a day. She just refused to do it. The lie of "I forgot" was easy for her to say. Ruth had become accustomed to saying, I forgot and that ends it. Once Barbara impressed upon her mother that the water was as important as the medicine, she did not hear "I forgot" again concerning the water. Of course, now Barbara is alerted that anything her mother does not want to do she says "I forgot." Barbara noticed that when Ruth truly forgets something, she becomes upset.

Amnesia is understandable. The person usually is struggling to remember or just moves on in life with whatever they remember. In the case of schizophrenia, who knows when the person remembers or copts out because "it wasn't me." The person commits the act and gets out of the way so that the other person can take the blame. Mentally sane individuals practice this behavior as well. Let's call it taking responsibility. If one is caught doing wrong, even in the act, the constant plea is "it wasn't me." Reversing the situation—something to be rewarded occurs and that same person was against it but he is the first to take credit.

5. Habitual Liars

Two words, mental illness. Habitual liars have a mental problem. They have developed the art of lying to the level at which they actually believe what they are saying and doing is true and truth. I included this poem to be a little clearer.

I came up with the wrong results, it doesn't fit
Yes, I am guilty again, I love it
They tell me to stop, forget it.
I lied about it, and that's it.

The reality of it is, these people are on the other end of "you cannot handle the truth." They create situations that they can benefit from through scams, schemes, and manipulations. Most times these people have relied on lies to successfully help them to achieve the results that they want. These can include: getting their way, winning an argument, being the center of attention, or in Donald's case, all of the above.

Case study:

Donald Brown, now deceased was a very bright and well mannered man. He was pleasant to be around and always positive and uplifting. It seems whenever and wherever you would see Donald, there was a degree of contentment he possessed that was immeasurable. He was comfortable in his own skin and the magnitude of lies he told were all beneficial and working for the good of Donald.

Donald needed money. Oh, let me enlighten you. Donald is a drug addict. Instead of robbing or stealing by the normal means. Donald did it this way. One whole day, Donald strolled up and down the streets in his mother's neighborhood professing that she had died and the family was struggling with the lack of money for her funeral. He was successful in acquiring the money.

You would think that after receiving money from this lie that Donald would not dare tell this lie again. What audacity, to think that this tight knit neighborhood, where everyone knew not only that his mother alive but that he was a drug addict would believe the same lie a few months later. Well, he was successful in receiving money again. Some of the same people were convinced that he was telling the truth this time. When the neighborhood discovered that they had been spoofed again, that his mother was live and well, everyone knew—including Donald that he would not be believed again about anything because he was now known as "the boy who cried wolf."

That is a dangerous situation to find yourself branded as a liar. Imagine if Patrick Henry had been branded a liar. When he warned the town folk that the British were coming, I doubt that anyone would have paid him any attention, unwittingly changing history.

6. Expert Liars

When we look at these liars you are perplexed, mesmerized, convinced, and persuaded. These expert liars can be any of the five liars discussed earlier as well as any combination. You will find these expert liars in professions such as salesmen, bill collectors, politicians, and lawyers to top the list. What you will notice about these professions is that each one requires the gift for gab, the ability to gain one's confidence and to take control.

Always to get the desired results involve a person telling another person just what they want to hear. It is easy to get someone on your side or doing what you want them to do if you are saying what they want to hear. Can that always be the truth? Well, as we have discussed previously a little something sprinkled into the truth will always make a lie.

It is obvious that it takes a lie in order to be good at any of the professions listed previously. I will outline a scenario for a salesperson.

Case study:

A telemarketer name Pete was on a call trying to sell some magazines. He went down the line starting with Parade and actually parading many others. With no success, Pete resorted to asking the potential buyer what he could do to get her to buy the magazines. The reply was "what else will I be getting for that price?" Quickly Pete said, "I'm sorry didn't I mention a bookcase comes along with the magazines." "No," the potential buyer happily answered. "In that case, I will be purchasing Parade."

The now buyer gave Pete an opportunity to lie and he took it. And, Pete ran with it. He racked up on sales that day, promising all the calls into those including book cases with the magazines. His sales stood out so much that one of the managers had to listen to his call to find out how did he improve his pitch so much from the night before. To Pete's surprise, he was fired. The lie that was paying off did not pay off in the end.

There are numerous expert lies and liars that are worth mentioning. One, I have included a short story, but a shorter similar case study follows.

Case Study:

Jackie caught a cab from school. As she sat down, she could not miss the photo of the driver directly to her left. When the driver turned around to ask her destination, Jackie immediately said "Who is that in the picture? Your brother?" The driver instantly responded, no that is my cousin. I could not find my picture today, so he let me borrow his.

While Jackie knew that the driver and the picture did not match, she could not be certain who the man in the picture was. While the driver very well could have been telling the truth he was living a lie. He obviously believed it to be a perfect lie up until Jackie confronted him. He did tell her, he was going home and finding his photo.

7. A Test For Perceived Liars (Check For Lies)

Once you believe someone is lying to you on a regular basis, test them. This test will protect you from potential distress and hurt. It could also protect your bank account.

First, ask a simple question regarding something that you had encountered with this person in the past and see if the answer coincides with how it was answered previously.

Next, if the answer is slow in coming, sound rehearsed, is totally different, or you do not get an answer instead a redirected response or argument you will get a clearer picture of the true person.

Then, call the person on it by telling them a simple story about the boy who called wolf. (Example given on page - case study about Donald..) For those of you who do not know the story, a boy was constantly running out telling everyone the wolf was coming when in fact the wolf was not coming. He was doing this just to tease, frighten, or maybe have fun with people....whatever his rationale when the wolf actually did come, nobody believed him.

Let the person know that it is important that you find them trustworthy, believable, and honest. Finally. Make it clear that you cannot have a relationship with someone who lies. Show them how if they lie about one thing you will always wonder what lie is coming next.

Now that you have given this test you have set the standards that you will and will not accept. Should the person continue acting suspiciously, deem that person a liar and not worthy of your trust and confidence.

Just think about it for a minute. Have you had a need to lie? Can you actually count the times you have lied? Do you regret any lies that you have told? Were those lies really necessary? Lies are misleading?

I asked myself those same questions since I am always the first to tell anyone, "I don't lie." Absolutely, I have found this statement to be a lie. For years, nobody could challenge me on that statement because I was an always tell the truth and never tell a lie" person, until recently.

My relationship with my husband is as honest a relationship as I could ever wished to embrace. Yet recently, he has been asking me the most difficult unimaginable questions. Once I hesitate and ponder, with a puzzled look on my face, he promptly says, "Now Ms. Banks, you don't lie." And, I am thinking "don't lie." But, the lie pops out.

The first time I lied to my husband, I couldn't believe it. Me, lying. Who is he? How did he get me to lie? It was all his fault. Nobody could have me take responsibility for lying. I was so angry with him for making me lie and with myself for lying. He asked me a question that irritated me. While he was joking but serious, I recall him saying "Ms. Banks, did you take your act-right medicine?"

Act-right medicine, act-right medicine, the term kept colliding with my emotions. The nerve of him asking me about taking medicine to make me act right. I didn't answer. I was thinking I am not going to answer. But he would not stop asking me. Over, and over. "Ms. Banks, did you take your act-right medicine."

Finally, I answered, vaguely "Yes." He quickly said "Good." That really got my goat. Daily, he would ask me the same question. Night and day. Until one day, I was fed up enough to tell the truth, "No, I did not take any act-right medicine. If acting right is doing what you expect me to do as opposed to doing what I do, I am never going to take it.

He still asks me, every now and then about that "act-right medicine." Now I have taken my position back on being truthful and I laugh and say "of course I did." You see now,

I do not perceive my response as a lie. I do not believe it qualifies.

Many of you, like myself, have feelers and what may be a lie to someone else certainly is not a lie to us...while we know, it is not the truth. So, somewhere in that grey area or what other color we want to call it other than black or white, right or wrong, truth or lie resides that place of safety where we say and do what we believe is the best thing for that situation.

Whether someone else accepts our behavior as truth or untruth (a lie) is completely their burden. Generally, we lie without thinking just to shut a person's mouth-----as in the case with my interactions with my husband. Off the cusp, we just may respond anyway. For example, should your husband or mate, parent, sibling, friend, or stranger ask you a question that you feel will be too much information for them or in other words none of their business, depending on several factors we may elect to say the first thing that pops into our head without any allegiance to it, not answer, or flatly say "It is none of your business."

The funny thing about telling someone close to you that it is none of their business usually gets a comeback of "it is my business." Crude as it sounds, respect for the presentation of that fact should let you know your boundaries. I have found that people have a "tit for tat" mentality. That is... "would tell you why won't you tell me. I did it why won't you do it."

I cannot understand why people invade your personal space, uniqueness, and individuality. Reasonable people appreciate and practice respect. And respect each other's differences in such a diverse society. A famous writer was said to have said something to this effect "....if you really listen you may very well hear the voice of God..." Not unlike God, I would like to be taken seriously. You don't have to kiss my feet thou or dry them with your hair, simply, **don't lie to me.**

In my conclusion I will replay what to look and listen for in detecting a lie.

1. **The credibility of the person**
2. **The believability of what is said.**
3. **Weigh the gains and losses.**
4. **Look for tell tell signs right then and in the near future.**

    a. **Fidgeting**
    b. **Sweating**
    c. **Stumbling**
    d. **nervousness, tense**
    e. **avoiding eye contact**
    f. **change in voice pitch**
    g. **a degree of urgency**

> h. and many more, but remember a good liar may have mastered all of the signs and lie sailing smoothly.

Also, you may want to try an exercise of asking the same thing several different ways to see if you get the same answer. Asking the questions at different time intervals is most effective.

Check for Lies

In checking for lies we can focus on things most often lied about and/or we can target people lied to most often. Word of mouth works for finding liars out as it does in advertising. Bad news travel fast. We see this everyday on the Internet with the amount of hits bad news gets. Exceptions always exist. But in most cases, if two or more people are in agreement you may want to pay attention and check the person out for yourself or better still, take their word for it if you do not have anything to lose.

Lies always come disguised. Lies can be beautiful, amazing, believable, convincing, emotional, necessary, unnecessary, and all the others I have listed and more. Tests for employment have a way of detecting if a person really knows the material or if they are guessing. It is conducted the same way you can reveal a liar — ask the same question multiple ways. Again be reminded that a person can make a mistake a lie because of false information they believe to be true.

There are at least 77 facts that once you hear them you will believe it to be a huge lie. One fact is (not on this list) is that when a men's store has a sale - 2 free suits when you buy one, is distorted and misleading. You are not getting a deal because the suits that you have to purchase before you get this deal are hard-to-sell, expensive suits. Also, the advertising brings you in the store and inevitably, you will buy something, mission accomplished.

To utilize your power once being assured of the decision you have made concerning a lie or the truth, forgive. Most times that forgive can involve moving on and out of that person's life.

8. Livers of Lies

Ask anyone who is living a lie if he/she is and the answer will be "no." In most instances, others can see people who living a lie, yet those who are living a lie are oblivious to it. I am sure you are familiar with the phrase "don't believe the hype." Well, that is exactly what has happened in this case. Self-talk has these individuals pumped up and they don't try to keep up with the Joneses, they have to beat the Joneses. In doing so, these people put themselves in awkward positions that result in their disappointments outweighing their achievements and possessions.

I have two case studies for your examination. If you know anyone who fits either of these studies, do what you can to assist them. In these cases, they are beyond anyone's help.

Case study:

Robert was raised in a sheltered environment with a rooster pecked mother and belligerent father. His mother showered him with all his desires and his father continued to raise the bar of expectations in every area. Now a successful young man, he reached for more than he could handle. Clothes, cars, furniture, travel, women were just a few of the things that he went overboard acquiring. While Robert had a wonderful job, he could not afford his lavish lifestyle. Whenever Robert would loose some possession he would replace it with a better one, he said "they are looking at me and expect me to have better and more than they do and I aim to please."

Robert purchased a home that he could not afford and each month had to borrow money from his mother to make the mortgage. Finally, the mother tired from appeasing her son and told him to find a wife. Robert took her advice, found a woman who was making at least twice the salary he was making and married her. After 10 years of misery, he had a remodeled house with no resemblance of himself, more bills, and no wife. He has now learned the lesson of living a lie.

Case study:

Cassie and her sister Bay lived with their mother, Kate and her boyfriend. Kate loves to cook. Every Sunday, Kate cooks the best dinners and quite a lot of food as well. Kate has company over and they eat until they are stuffed, while Cassie and Bay split a chicken wing.

If chicken is not on the menu, Cassie and Bay assume they are vegetarians. Both Cassie and Bay remember this as if it was yesterday when it was over 40 years ago. It is the culprit that has them living a lie.

Cassie always buys the biggest and the best. She has a wonderful job but she has to continue working long after she can retire due to health issues. She cannot afford to retire.

When Bay retired, she had two automobiles and was too ill to drive either. Her bills were piling up and she was faced with the option of moving to a smaller home or getting a part-time job for the second time after retirement. All in all. Both Cassie and Bay brag about their childhood and how their mother cooked three meats each Sunday.

While this may very well be true, Cassie and Bay benefitted little from it. Cassie says that is why she always cooks three meats on Sunday because that is what she is used to having. "I do not remember it that way. Cassie." says Bay. It is a lie.

Bay on the other hand, simply looks down on other people whether they are doing well or not. Bay wants to be looked up to and somehow believes that she can get this adoration and respect if she treats people the way she perceives she was treated. Bay believes she is better than everyone else—smarter (with no real formal education and training) more beautiful (with no real facial or inner beauty) and richer (with one investment and no real money). Bay also, is living a lie.

Regina's Box

Have you gotten this far in life and not heard of the mythological "Pandora's Box"? In short, everything evil was in it. One account of the tale tells of how hope was in there and got out and the other account tells how hope was in there and did not get out.

Regina's Box is the box of hope. All good things are in this box and when you meet Regina you can make a list yourself. This box of hope is filled with hope, faith, truth, honesty, integrity, love, kindness, helpfulness, service, warmth, sweetness, support, dependability, knowledge, humility, generosity, thoughtfulness, and goodwill.

Unlike Pandora's box that was not supposed to be opened but was opened, Regina's box should be opened and remain open. Utilizing those things in Regina's box will diffuse a lie and most times produce a confession to the truth.

9. Putting Lies To Rest

It is an easy thing to do when you make up your mind. Put those lies to rest. Is it you who is doing the lying? Is it someone else who is doing the lying? Can it be that you both are making your case and the liar has to be chosen? (Your word against mine.) Regardless, whoever is lying stop it. It takes too much energy.

There are times when you may tell a person anything to get them out of your face, off your phone, or out of your hair. You are lying but you got rid of them for that moment. That person may have been hounding you or that person may have been whining and begging for your approval or support about a situation. You could have agreed with them just to shut them up and move on to something else. Whatever the case, you must stand firm on the truth at any cost because the situation can arise at a later date and when you take the stand that you should have taken then...why now, it sounds like you are lying.

Witnesses_in court sessions take the stand and take an oath to tell the truth. Should they lie and get caught, they are charged with perjury. When the defendant or plaintiff takes the oath they can either lie or tell the truth as well, although they are sworn to tell the truth.

They are told to tell the truth, the whole truth, and nothing but the truth. It seems that the truth cannot be anything but the whole truth. In addition, they have to take the oath on the holy bible. Do we even know if the person respects the Bible? What allegiance do they have to it?

So many things in our lives depend heavily on whether we are getting the truth or something else, a lie. I have heard so many people say (and I have said it myself) "I was as truthful as I could be. Meaning they could have said,more or they could have lied.

Run Tell That

One very dark and rainy night, I was driving my 1994 Camaro from Washington, D.C. to Baltimore with my cousin Elaine on my way to my sister's Gail's Birthday dinner at a restaurant. After being seated, I noticed my cousin Elaine seemed uncomfortable. Most of the people who were at the rather long table were strangers to the both of us. My sister was a little intoxicated and did a lot of laughing and talking to them and kept repeating "where's my birthday present?" Making a long story short. After dinner, I am driving home in the horrible rainstorm. I could not see anything. Elaine kept complaining about being ignored and feeling left out at the dinner. I said I felt the same way, just to shut her up. I was trying to focus on the road and was tired of her whining.

Well, two years later, my sister and I are visiting Elaine at her home. My sister invites her to a birthday party at her home. Our cousin, Elaine says, "I will never come to a birthday party of yours after the way you treated me last time. Diann and I both felt ignored." My sister, stunned says to me "Is that right?" I answered "No." My cousin lost it. She began shouting "I cannot believe you are backing down to your sister. I never thought I would see the day that you would back down to anyone." Now, my sister is perplexed. She thinks I am lying while I was lying two years ago not thinking that something like that would ever come up to be addressed.

Nevertheless, my cousin was upset with me and I explained it to my sister later. She said she understood, but did she? That lesson taught me not to go along with anyone if I did not agree because that would clearly make me a liar at some point.

Many times you and I may alter a fact intentionally or unintentionally based on our personal interpretation or/and bias. When we have that wavering room we certainly will swing some obscure facts in our direction. An example of this follows in a case study.

Case Study:

"Our selection process involves discovering the candidate's dedication to their platform." said the chief judge. Gloria, (a candidate) upon hearing this, immediately changed her platform from the specific and clear "helping others" to the broad and obscure "healthcare". While her rationale was centered on being selected, she had gotten off track because "helping others" was her dedication unlike "healthcare" her interpretation of what the greater subject that the majority of people may have been biased towards. An action and spoken word of deceit, a lie, that caused Gloria to miss the mark.

As Gloria played the guessing game and moved in the wrong direction, we so often throw in our good hands of honesty to tell a lie that we believe will produce the most benefits. Solely, we must consider what we say and do in all our endeavors and relationships disallowing a lie to override our truth.

Our truth again does not necessarily justify the truth. Everyone has a point of view. What may be true to you may not ring true to another. In particular cases such as this, what is the truth — in a debate setting, who is telling the truth, the whole truth, and nothing but the truth? On the other side of the coin, the other person is telling a lie? No. Not in all cases.

Case Study:

Two friends, Joel, Sammie, and Sara, (Sammie's sister) watched a movie about wild animals. Both Joel and Sammie love animal movies. Sara was expecting an independent movie unlike the one she saw with her brother and his friend. When Sammie and Sara's father, Denver asked the three young people what they thought of the movie, you can imagine where the difference of opinions. Undoubtedly, Joel and Sammie loved the movie though Sara's disappointment overshadowed her judgment, Sara intelligently formulated an answer spoke from the point of view of how the movie was produced. She went into detail about the scenery and the direction of the plot. Finally, Sara faintly and playfully shouted out "hated it." So, based on their answers, Denver responded, "I don't think I want to watch the movie. I know that Sara doesn't like animals but she didn't like anything about the movie. You know I respect all of your opinions, but Joel and Sammie, you two would love any movie with animals."

While Denver drew a conclusion based on his knowledge of the three young people, telling them how much he respected their opinions, any one of them could have been lying. Joel and Sammie may very well just wanted to agree, therefore pleasing each other. And Sara, could have just been contrary because she assumed that would be the anticipated response everyone wanted to hear.

In the event Denver watches the movie and agrees with Sara. He may attack Joel and Sammie telling them they lied about the movie. He didn't love it or think it was a good movie. Denver thought they possibly lied about the movie, but then again, it was just their opinion.

Matters such as the one just stated does not really make a big difference to result in any damaged outcome. They were asked a simple question "Was this a good movie?" A simple yes or no may have sufficed for some, while on another level a more detailed response may have been required.

Remember, different opinions may result in different answers but unconditionally can result in the same answers. Varied answers may still equate to the answers in agreement, but none of these can be classified as a lie.

10. Who Wants To Hear It

Lies right? Wrong. People seem not to want to hear the truth. They believe that most cannot handle the truth. The practice of watering down or sweetening a statement tends to make the statement a "little white lie." A lie is a lie. Validation of this is an effort to easing one's pain or softening the blow.

Many people are uncomfortable accepting and even expressing something good has happened to them. Somehow they believe they are being boastful and cocky and should be exhibiting humbleness and meekness. The truth of something is just that. While the people who are possessing the good news cannot properly display their happiness, they also cannot convey it and sometimes others cannot receive it.

Generally, down playing good news serves both the person with the good news as well as the person receiving it.

"When it is about me I don't want to be puffed up and when someone is hearing it about me I tell them I really didn't deserve it." In fact, you did deserve it and to not puff yourself up, you tell a lie. Why? To make someone think more of you and not resent you or become jealous of you. There are so many reasons to lie but know are justified. In the end, the truth wins.

Good news. So, are we stuck between a rock and a hard place? Do we continue to lie because at the time it seems to make life easier or do we tell the truth always and confront whatever lies or trues they bring?

The answer is simple. Be true to yourself. If you tell lies, for whatever reason, then you are what you say and do. I know that you will feel better about yourself if you can look at yourself in the mirror and be proud that you stand for the truth. I know that you will feel better about yourself because people say you are nothing but the truth.

11. The Need To Lie

Fudging is the tool used to fix or right a mistake or a wrong doing. While fudging is a wrongdoing it serves to alter and adjust the truth. Numbers are frequently fudged to balance totals as well as project the results that you desperately need. Accountants may have to shift numbers in their calculating as well as everyday people when there I a desire to get a tax refund.

Whenever there is a need to lie, it should be for the protection of the person. A situation may occur when it is a matter of life or death and the only recourse available is lying. This is the time that resolution depends on a well constructed lie. The intent of lying is mainly a safety device not a practice.

Lying is useful when it benefits you if you are under any type of duress and/or danger. Encouraging you to lie is not my intent rather an alternative when you have little or no choice in overcoming an obstacle.

For instance, it may be that there is a gun to your head and someone is asking "Do you love me? If you say no, I will kill you." While this seems far fetched, it is an everyday occurrence. It may not be a gun to the head rather the consequences of a gun to the head. Many times in abusive relationships, a lie is the abused one's best friend.

I remember being told two different things at two separate times. First I was told a lie is a lie. Second I was told I should tell a little white lie. Well, my explanation of why I lied brought about "a lie is a lie". But, when I hurt someone's feelings with a true response, I was later told that in those types of cases, I had permission to soften the blow—not to say exactly what I was thinking or feeling. I did not like the difference then now do I like it now.

Instead of softening the blow with a half truth, I prefer not to say anything or to say you don't want to know (you don't want me to tell you.) Now that I have been using Regina's box it is becoming easier and more pleasant to tell people what they don't want to hear but they asked.

There will be those you know who don't have time to hear or see how truthful you are or how well you are doing. When you tell them that all is well with you they cannot stand it. Do not align yourself with these people. You want to be around positive, honest people who wish you the best and will accept nothing but the best from you.

The young people have a saying "word is bond." The old people have been saying "you are as good as your word."

Therefore, if your word is no good neither are you any good. It has been said for years that a good name is better than gold. Your character. Everyone knows that the best advertisement is "word of mouth." If everyone is talking about you and it is good, you can go a long way with people. On the other hand, should everyone who talks about you consider you a liar, then people will try to be a long way from you.

Integrity will take you a long way. It is something that people can witness. When you make commitments you follow through. When you make promises you see them through. And when you have a certain character that character shows up. You are solid. Only when you profess one thing and show something else will people see you as not being trustworthy. You must be dependable and true if that is your claim. Those qualities must present themselves otherwise you will be seen as a fake, a liar.

Associating with liars will shed a bad light on you. Those who know them as liars will take for granted that you are okay with the liars and that you may even be a liar yourself. Your reputation is important. Who wants to hear good news? Only those people who want you to be successful and truthful will be truthful with you. In some cases, the truth may hurt, but the truth actually will make you free.

12. Ordinary Lies
(Typical lies)

Stereotypes is a huge lie. We are all familiar with the many stereotypes associated with race. I want to look at the stereotype of "the married man." Wives overall seem to give the same advice to each other. This ranges from newly weds to golden anniversary wives. In their conversations about their husbands, they say "all of them are like that, all of them do that." Well, the wives who are looking for solutions to correct the disorder and disruption in their homes do not accept those empty responses.

All and none are definite lies. Should wives just roll over and accept undesirable behavior from their husbands, based on these type of lies, will not have the quality of life they planned. Unknowingly, the wives who adopt the stereotype of the married man is settling for less than she deserves. In the long run, she is defeated because unacceptable behavior has become something that she feels cannot be changed rather tolerated. It becomes the norm because everybody else says it.

Husbands on the other hand, when they discuss their wives with other husbands will get a similar stereotype of "the married woman." "All of them nag and complain, they are crazy." These are just a few of the remarks these newly wed and golden anniversary husbands proclaim about their wives. Again, all and none are lies. There are many exceptions to the rule.

To dig deeper. Is it warranted? In speaking with over 100 married men about their relationships with their wives, once they voice their frustrations and listen to suggestions it is clear that they were accepting the behavior as well. These men did not consider the fact that they could actually do and say things that would change their wives nagging and complaining. And oh yes, craziness. When these men were asked if they brought their wive's craziness to their attention, they said "of course, and she said "you make me crazy" or "you are the one who is crazy." My favorite response was "I was not crazy until I met you."

1

Sometimes before a person can ask another person a question, he can expect a lie. While the answer may in fact be the truth, it can pose some uncertainty or doubt. The determining factors are if, what, who, how much, what if, how about you believe. I have done the work for you, do not factor in if or anything other than what is otherwise you have changed the situation. You are questioning something which leads to the believe-ability of the situation relenting any contributing factors such as credibility and/or connection with the person

Most typical lies are ones that we expect. You might say they come with the territory. For example, a poker game and even black jack. When you are trying to win, you project confidence, certainty, positivity, as to see what the other player(s) or dealer is projecting. Most times in black jack you can more easily be shut down by the deal or by your decision. In Poker you have a better and longer time to bluff or examine the player(s) eithr way, you may be on either side of a lie. You are expected to be a hustler in these situations. Many utilize these practices in all they do. This could be lie is projecting and then deciding if you are going to make a decision on what you know, what you think, or what you will take a chance on.

It is funny when people first meet and for at least two months of the initial meeting people tend to send their representative that usually is not the same person they are. You are doing the same, sending your representative, but you and the representative are one in the same. When that does not exist in your relationship with another person, you have the option of denying that truth and getting on that person's level to deal with them or live responsibly and stay away from toxic people when you have the choice between breathing and enjoying your life, stress and drama free; or chose a lie.

Time Always Tells On Liars

In a matter of time, you will see if a person is believing that acting serves them well. Now the faking continues but now you are sure that what you have been hearing and seeing does not match up. When you understand who is coming for dinner, you simply need to regret when something toxic is inevitable.

Don't spare another's feelings at the risk of putting yourself at risk of stress, ulcers, heart attack, stroke, or worst. Who can discover, catch, or expose a liar better than time. I wrote a poem about it.

Who tells on a liar?
Time will tell.
Is one the loneliest number?
Only time will tell.

Time is the teller of all things.
You can bank on time.
He shows up right on time.
You can bank on time.

As we know, many times people send their representative to meet you. They know who you are what you will accept and they give you what you want. After no more than three months, you meet the real person. And, in some cases up to three years as in this short story.

I Am Pretty And Smart

Emma, Ms. Senior DC 2011 performed as Michael Jackson. She was 3 years older than me, tight body, and could move. I do believe she was the best choice. Nonetheless, I know and everybody agreed that she made a better queen than any of us could have made. This, Emma (Michael Jackson) loudly told a huge lie on me in my face. I kept asking her over and over and she kept lying to me about what I had not done. I went into detail and she continued to say "I didn't know anything about it." (First she would not have been there if she did not know anything about it. — I was not going to have a congratulatory lunch with our group and not invite the queen. How dare she say that she didn't know about it The purpose of the lunch was to build a team so that we could support the queen and each other.

Well, I cried and told her not to ever speak to me again. The room was upset, I got in her face and told her if she would lie in my face there is no telling what kinds of lies she would make up. I made sure everybody understood that Emma was no longer permitted to say anything to me. That way nobody would believe her if she had any story with my name it. That was wonderful for me. Everybody wanted my position once they found out for themselves that she was a liar and some other things that were in Pandora's box.

Well I took the time out to observe her because there were clearly two separate people I had encountered. Just yesterday, I got my answer. (I stopped speaking to her in July 2011 and began speaking to her in September 2013) She thinks she has a right to do and say whatever she pleases whenever she pleases and she is not being rude or interrupting. She is right and everybody else is wrong and she doesn't care what they think because everybody is jealous of her brains and beauty.

Should Emma ever tell a lie on me, then I am slipping. I know better than to put myself in that situation. I had several witnesses at the 2011 incident and it still was a noncommittal response from them until I made them come face to face with the truth. They knew if they had not told the truth, I would stop talking to them as well. We're all in the same club. It just looks so much better when senior citizens behave well.

Emma approached me and told me that the reason people had a problem with her was because she was pretty and smart. She said that her grandmother told her when she was a child that people would have a problem with her throughout her life because she was pretty and smart.

The following are some typical questions and believe it or not answers. You decide, could be the truth — could be a lie.

1. Q. Are you married?

      A. Yes.

      B. No.

      C. I was.

      D. He is.

      E. Thirty years.

Any of the above answers can be true as well as a lie. Skipping A and B, the yes and no answers. Starting with C, I was. What does that really mean? Left as is one can assume, no. It seems like no longer. It also could mean to that person that I no longer live as a married person (left the home but still married). I am waiting for my final papers. I have not filed for divorce yet. When a person responds this way, you must ask for clarity otherwise you my be left with a lie. The D response of "He is". May be interpreted as I am not legally divorced but it is over for me, but my husband still considers us married. In fact, D is still married. Lastly, E states "thirty years." He may be telling a lie just to establish credibility but on the other hand telling the truth about being married, but in name only (he has not lived as man and wife with his wife for more than 28 years—just neither he or his wife ever bothered to get a divorce).

2. Q. How old are you?

    A. The correct age

    B. A flattering age

    C. Refuse to answer

    D. How old do I look?

    E. How old are you?

All of the answers excluding A border on a possible upcoming lie or lie. B is a solid lie, C is a coming attraction for a lie, D and E tends to provoke empathy; it is an effort to give you an answer that you are anticipating; a pleasing acceptable answer.

Women more than men are guilty of either putting their age up or down. Readily, we know why women would put their age down but up? You see, when a woman says, "I am 77" and in reality she is only 63, the compliments pour in. "You look great for 77; I hope I look as good as you when I am your age; You skin is so beautiful, etc." On the other hand, when women put their age down it is usually by a few years. While, my friend Brenda loves to celebrate her birthday by saying "I am 29." One year, her daughter, Ella was 29. I thought no way will Brenda continue to play with this and not reach 30. To this day, each birthday, Brenda smiles, laughs and says "I'm 29."

3. How much do you weigh?

A cut and dry question such as this invokes evasiveness and the results from the survey were 90 percent, "I don't know" responses.

The following questions are ones that you can answer as well as I can. They are here to remind you of how shallow people can be when they are put in a position to tell the truth.

4. Do you have children or how many children do you have?
5. Did you finish school or how much education do you have?
6. What do you do? (Where do yo work, what type of work?)
7. How do you feel (happy, sad, upset; hot, cold, hungry; etc.)?
8. Are there any questions?
9.
10. Was it good? (A meal, movie, a performance of yours, sex...)
11. Did you complete that task?

The importance of the question as well as who is asking the question always determines the response. Importance is relative. Therefore, the urgency and need for the truth is dependent on how much weight one places on the question as well as how much weight one places on the person who is asking the question.

Number 9 (Do you understand?) is a very dangerous question to lie about. Many people are embarrassed to admit that they do not understand something. Later, when put to the test it could prove a disaster to either side.

Lying in the face of many typical questions (of which the list is limitless and not all listed here) can be natural and automatic. Effortlessly, without giving any or much thought to the lie, a person will respond shamelessly. These are called open-faced lies as well as bald faced lies. It takes the cake when a person lies to you on you to your face, as demonstrated in the previous story, "I Am Pretty And Smart".

Fights and sometimes fatalities result from these types of lies. Taking back the lie or asking for forgiveness can diffuse many of these situations. You will find that the liars refuse to confess or admit the lie.

In most cases, the lie is not one that is seen to warrant much consequence. You undoubtedly have been a witness to a typical lie either on one side of it or the other.

When a question is asked about a person's feelings or what a person is feeling, controversy can easily be stirred up. Here is another short story.

Play Along Or Leave

Gwen was sitting in a room and she was really hot. It was summer and the room was steaming. All the windows were shut tight; no air-conditioning; no fans; no ventilation. Two other people were in the living room with Gwen, Dottie and Ethel.

Gwen clamored, "Is anybody else hot or just me?" Ethel tried to quiet Gwen down with a sharp look and a tone of I agree but her words were "Just you!" "Actually, I feel a little chilly." When Gwen continued to complain about the heat, Ethel politely invited her to leave. Well, the situation was simply this. Dottie was in her last stage of cancer and was cold. Ethel endured the heat so that Dottie would be comfortable. In fact, the heat was turned on. Ethel told a lie to Gwen that she was not hot and told a lie to Dottie that she was also cold.

An incident like this clarifies and justifies the exception of lying. This signifies sacrifice and goodwill. Love always points us in the direction to do the best thing in a hard situation and if it requires lying then lie.

There is a popular saying "If you will lie, you will steal; if you will steal, you will kill." This saying has been used over the years to encourage young children to tell the truth. Another popular saying is "Honesty is the best policy." Well neither statement is flawless. Starting with the later we have seen, just in the last scenario how honesty would not have been the best policy. Gwen kept Dottie at ease and as stress free as possible. Dottie had certainly enough to think about in her last days than to have to add to her condition that Gwen was hot and uncomfortable.

Considering the many facets of what lies really mean, I am sure you can tell a story that is absolutely hilarious from your point of view that is terribly painstaking from someone else's point of view. Who is the liar? Understanding and forgiveness are tools that provide an appropriate settlement for lies and/ or liars. Given the correct amount of information, one can evaluate a lie and/or liar fairly.

When you find out or are found the liar, forgiveness plays a gigantic role. Forgiving yourself, forgiving others. Parents have taken children from their children and kept the children right in the family and the family lives that lie.

I remember when Ruth found out she was adopted. She turned on her adopted parents and told me they had lied to her. She was three years older than I was but I didn't see that as a lie. Is it?

13. Why Lie?

Individual	Gender	Age	Reason to Lie
Erin	Female	17	No reason to lie
Tanya	Female	56	To keep peace
Esther	Female	65	When things are personal
Tim	Male	32	To stay keep out of trouble
Patrice	Female	24	It's fun; fooling people
LaVonne	Female	22	To fit in
Roger	Male	28	Because I don't get caught
Thomas	Male	84	What's the point?
Lilly	Female	70	When I feel I'm in danger
Charles	Male	10	So I won't get a beating
Tracey	Female	44	To pass a customer service exam
Brandy	Female	35	There is no reason to lie
Eric	Male	37	I just decline answering
Elizabeth	Female	51	I lie all the time (only little ones)
William	Male	17	I do it to get along with my friends
Benjamin	Male	89	I try not to lie, don't always make it

In conducting a survey regarding why an individual lies, you just reviewed the findings on the previous page. Lying comes easily to some and takes a lot of energy for others. Conscience plays a major role in choosing whether to lie or not lie. From the table you can assess that the majority of the people survey confessed to lying. One respondent's answer was particularly interesting. He said "I try not to lie but I don't always make it." That is the place I believe we all should aspire toward. Years of observation has shown me that the truth certainly does make you free.

The truth makes you free from worry–worrying about if you will get caught in the lie; if you are going to tell more lies to defend and support the original lie; And, free from guilt-the guilt of I should have told the truth.

Some results that I did not record are how the lie makes you feel. Approaching this from the common denominator in all the responses, I summed it up as "power." Controlling what a person says to another is totally within their power. Timid and meek types lie as well and as much as bold and forward types. The bold and forward types are predicted to be more susceptible to lying while the timed and meek slip through the cracks are overlooked because of the course of action they take when they lie. Most times their lies are more calculating and penetrating. Although I cannot give any credence to this statement, I can give an example of how the outspoken comes under attack and is given less credit for being truthful or anything else positive for that matter than the shy, withdrawn, quiet timid liar.

There are people whose friends love and understand that are described this way "if you don't want to know, don't ask him/her." Well, this does not mean that they are liars rather the opposite. They are straight shooters and will tell you the truth without any filters, whether you like it or not. These people speak up for themselves, situations, and other people.

Associates, bosses, and others who do not know these people may speak of these same people this way. — "Empty borrows make the most noise." or something to that effect, implying that they really do not have anything to say. Discounting the credibility of these people who will not go along with a program or concept that does not sit right with them. Most, not all, timid and meek–shy, withdrawn, quiet people will go along with the program even if they disagree thus clearly lying to themselves and others whereby making themselves guilty of being liars. These same people will beat you up and down that they do not lie. Unknowingly to themselves that if they do not take a stand for what they really believe then they are lying.

I will give you an example of an outspoken person who could not be heard, taken seriously, or respected because of their honesty. Another Short story.

Is Lying the Better Policy?

Tony, the supervisor of shipping, asked his employee Frankie a question that Tony already knew how Frankie would reply. Surprisingly, Frankie's response was not the intended response. Angrily, Tony spoke "Frankie, I didn't understand a word you said." Tony had not *heard* a word Frankie said because of his anticipation. Frankie, not being a mind reader, thought maybe I didn't speak clearly enough. Frankie answered again. This time he took time and enunciated every word. Since Frankie's answer was not what Tony wanted to hear, he simply stared at Frankie and said nothing. Frankie left the room, he feeling castrated. A bright idea popped in his head, "I will join a speaking group. I am going to improve my speech. Nobody is going to tell me that they cannot understand what I am saying, again".

Frankie joined a self-help group, excelled in booth communications and leadership. Seven years later, Frankie is on a new job with a new supervisor, Hank. Hank called Frankie into his office and gave him a performance evaluation. He told Frankie how pleased he was with his work and no matter how much he did or how well he did it, there was no advancement for him there. Frankie smiled and said, "No incentive." Hank instantly said, "What did you say?" Frankie repeated, "No incentive." Hank then replied, "You really have a way with words."

At the sound of this Frankie was reminded of what had happened seven years earlier with Tony. A light bulb came on in his head and he realized, my truth and integrity is killing me. Just the day before Frankie's friend Terry told him, you are going in for your evaluation tomorrow and it won't be good although you are the best worker here. Frankie asked Terry what he knew. And Terry responded "you don't know how to lie." Only liars get ahead here.

Now we know that Hank expected Frankie to get upset or maybe angry and ask why. Why am I not going to advance if you say that I am doing a great job? Frankie could have very well been upset or even angry but he was more appreciable of the truth so that he would not have to continue to go above and beyond expecting advancement that he was not going to receive.

14. Action Lies

There are so many ways people lie when their actions do not match up with their words. I can start with something as simple as when people quote scripture from the Bible saying "I can do all things through Christ which strengthens me." Try asking them something and they will be the first ones to tell you they cannot do it. And the reasons can consist of too busy............to........I don't know how to do it, among a million other explanations.

What you see is sometimes unbelievable and very well should be because it could be an illusion (a lie) or it can be the truth a fact. Is it a fact that the woman who is holding a sign saying "HOMELESS, CAN YOU GIVE ME MONEY FOR FOOD" really homeless? And, does she want food or money?

A woman asked a lady, a little ahead of me on the streets, for money for food. The woman went into a deli and came back quickly with a sandwich. The woman became belligerent and told the lady she did not want the sandwich. Confused and hurt, the lady said "I thought you were hungry." The woman replied, "Read the sign."

What you read can be fact, then again can you believe everything that you read?

I could never give you the whys to when the words and actions and actions and words do not line up but I certainly have some intriguing stories to tell. Here are just a few:

You Mean It

There was a misunderstanding between twin brothers, Claud and Clarence. They both knew a Carol, a dancer and were present at her dance recital. After the recital Clarence went up to Carol to congratulate her and pass on some referral information. Claud interrupted the two and gave his congratulations to Carol. While Clarence had more to say to Carol, he had completed the main business of the referral and he walked off with his brother. In the reception area, Carol catches up with Clarence again and they begin to pick up where they had left off. This time Claud begins to speak to Carol completely off the subject. Infuriated, Clarence says to Claud, "we are talking." Claud wisks off in a huff and goes to the back of the reception area. Carol asks Clarence what just happened and Clarence said he didn't know. Claud returns and Carol immediately excuses herself.

The twins eat a meal together and then they go their separate ways. Every morning Claud and Clarence are on the phone for about an hour but days pass without either one calling the other. One afternoon, Claud calls Clarence. "Hi Clarence, this is Claud." as if Clarence did not know who was on the other end of the line. "Clarence, I did not like the way you treated me at the recital. We both know Carol and I thought we were all talking." said Claud. "Well, Claud, I know Carol a lot better than you do and we were not all talking. You were being rude." Clarence sighed. "You see Clarence, I don't like the way you talk to me. Whenever I say anything to you about how you make me feel you always tell me –that's just the way you are... and I am telling you that is why I stay away and don't call you because I don't like the way you talk to me." chimed Claud. "I don't blame you Claud, if someone spoke to me in a way that I didn't like all the time and made me feel the way I didn't want to feel all the time, I would not speak to them or be bothered with them if I were you." Clarence exclaimed. Claud said, oh, okay and then hung up.

Clarence was so angry after the call. He could not believe that Claud was not acknowledging his rudeness and apologizing instead looking for an apology from him. From the conversation, Clarence did not expect to hear from Claud any time soon. He certainly was not going to call him and why would Claud call him, after all, Claud did not like the way Clarence talked to him ever.

A few weeks passed and Claud called. Clarence did not answer. Claud left a message, over and over again, all after call. Clarence did not answer. What could Claud possibly want? The last message from Clarence stated "I got it." And Clarence was hoping, I hope he got the fact that he was wrong and he said he did not like the way I talked to him so why is he calling me to talk to him.

In "You Mean It" it shows how a person can say one thing and do something else. I commend Clarence on sticking it out and allowing Claud to hear what he said and possibly see what he had done. Clearly, Clarence was okay with how Claud felt he just wanted to make him a believer instead of a liar.

The next story is entitled, "Don't Leave Me Out." It is about a young girl who is always the victim in her mind. This story as well teaches a lesson.

Don't Leave Me Out

Linda invited Cindy to a flower arrangement workshop. Cindy didn't readily say yes or no to the invitation but answered she would try to make it. Linda had invited Cindy to several of these workshops in the past and Cindy was not able to attend therefore when Linda saw Cindy entering the room, she was very honored and grateful. Before the workshop concluded, Cindy told Linda that she could not stay for the reception. While Linda was dismayed she thanked Linda for supporting her at the workshop. Joyce and Faye hurriedly followed Linda downstairs to the reception and preceded in setting the tables with an assortment of delicacies. To Linda's surprise, Cindy came down and asked if she could assist them. Linda responded, of course, and Linda moved forward greeting and serving the other guests.

That evening Cindy called Linda and cried out "I will never come to anything you host again. You ignored me." Linda did not know what to say and she said nothing. Cindy continued to murmur on and on about Linda's mistreatment of her and Linda remained silent. The telephone conversation ended.

Cindy arrived late to the workshop and had planned to leave before the reception began. Once she saw that she was not needed she felt a need to be needed. The lie was clearly that she had to leave because she did not leave.

Other actions that prove to be lies are:

1) The giving or acceptance of an engagement ring with no intentions of marrying the person.

2) Moving in with a person under the promise of marriage with no intent of marriage.

3) Borrowing money, clothes, household items etc. knowing that these things will not be returned.

4) Taking credit or ownership of something that is not yours.

5) Doing something that you don't have to do and don't want to do.

6) Following a belief that you do not share.

7) Insisting that a person remembers incidents that did not happen.

These are a few instances of action lies. Others are cheating on tests, etc. Obviously, when one cheats he/she is aware while in situations like number 7 on the previous page, a person can lie about something that they wanted to happen with another person that never happened becomes the truth the them. They have told the lie so much to themselves and other people that they believe it to be the truth.

15. What To Do

Many times people do not know what to do nor do they know what to say. We do the best we can to please others. Theses is actually a people type called a "people pleaser". In our world, another phrase for this is "a Polly anna". Theses people are not "I'm okay, You're okay" people. Instead of striving for balance in their relationships, their focus is dependant upon how another person feels.

Not only are these types concerned about how that person feels, also it is imperative that the person acknowledges that, should they feel "great", the Polly anna type made it happen. Whatever it takes, the Polly anna type's mission is to please you. Means, measures, circumstances, obstacles—all, Polly anna will overtake to accomplish the goals of pleasing someone. A popular quote, "by any means necessary". certainly is appropriate here. Seems like a good fit for a lie as well, you think? Well, this type feels an intense obligation to please. It is a duty.

Being obligated to another can cause a person to say they will do something they do not want to do or/and go somewhere when they do not want to go. Whether it be an in-crowd situation or a one-on-one situation, its dangerous. Once people become dependent on you due to the amount of times you have been there for them, the range of things you have done for them, or/and the number of years you have been performing the beckon call duties where does that leave you?

Most times you begin to become overwhelmed, exhausted, reluctant, and most of all resentful. All these negative things weighing on you that you caused in the first place. Take the blame! You did it to yourself. Thinking you could take care of another person's needs at the expense of neglecting your own serves disastrously. Nobody benefits in the long-run.

Case Study:

Three individual women; three separate stories; one shared theme. In the interest of time details will serve better than well defined characters and names. Woman 1: Gave all her time, money, and energy to her ailing mother (her siblings hung back and watched); Woman 2: Took care of her alcoholic sister's children as well as their children (as well as her sister when she was in transition); Woman 3: Oversaw the well-being of her mother, father, sisters, brothers, their children, her children, her children's friends, her friends, neighbors, strangers (from the cradle to the grave). All of these women share the same opinion about what and why they did what they did. Thank you was never a concern for them. They believed they were doing what they had to do and nobody could do it but them.

Just what they all said they did not need, they did not get. Instead they got a "who asked you and who cares response." After a combined time count of 150 years of selfless service, their responses are as follows: Woman 1: "If I hit the lottery, I am going to pay off all my siblings mortgages."; Woman 2: "Only one of my sister's children speaks to me. The other five, their children and my sister are all angry with me and refuse to associate with me.'" Woman 3: "I got it."

While you may tell yourself that you are doing something for someone because there is a need, somebody has to do it, you should do it (it's your Christian duty), or whatever reason you feel that you are within your right to go out of your way to do something nice for someone, visualize yourself in that situation and the re-evaluate the feasibility. Sure you still may proceed, but it is unlikely that you will go overboard regretting poor decisions in the future.

What we need to do, in every situation, is to be true to ourselves. Be honest. We can prevent depression, high blood pressure, stress, ulcers, strokes, and heart attacks simply by being honest. Integrity and trustworthiness are character treasures that may be productive in many instances and unproductive in few, stand to build the relationships that will last a lifetime. It has been said the greatest need of humans is the need to belong or be accepted.

The main ingredient that makes up a status seeker is the need to belong. Status seekers take it several steps further because they not only want to belong to a particular group whether it be social, spiritual, professional – they want to be looked up to, in charged, or the leaders.

Their prominence in the group leaves no room for question as to why they are there or should they be there. Chiseled in stone with no room to doubt, status seekers are known to do whatever it takes to achieve their goals. Make no mistake about it, lying is not left out of the formula.

This one need becomes the driving force behind so much deception. Status seekers must keep up the appearances that delivers them the satisfaction and acceptance they need. Once a factor falters that causes the status seeker to fall out of favor with the group such as loss of income, a spouse, some possession, even health or personal appearance— then another type of lying is inevitable.

Along with the new lies comes an unflattering image of denial. Earlier I mentioned this old saying "If you will lie, you will steal and if you will steal you will kill." Most times rather than to lose face with their peers, status seekers will resort to suicide. Somewhere between the lies and suicide there had to be some type of stealing. (Another issue for another time.)

I do believe that when we feel in good in our own skin we can come clean and be honest with others. If we have built up good solid relationships, a little fudging will in no way damage your image and another person's opinion.

We can do all the things that we know are right and go by every letter in the book; we can have the credentials, the enthusiasm and desire, and all the other necessary criteria points to enter into a group. This being said, does this give us the security we need to be comfortable and accepted by the group?

Insecurities will cause people to lie and then live to make that lie the truth. I have found it is easier to hold on to the truth because you don't have to think about it, it is similar to breathing or your reflexes. While a lie dictates that you have a good memory. Judge Judy said, "You have to have a good memory to tell a lie." She was pointing to the fact that the gentleman's written and oral complaint did not coincide. Yes, he had written one thing and was saying something different.

Acceptable behavior is what we need to practice. Lying can be devastating and result in many failed relationships.

Could Not Resist The Lie

Kenneth and Edward were newly weds of nine months. They moved into a wonderful new house in a new development and were ready to begin their exclusive lives together. Kenneth was a bowler and very active in the community, while Edward on the other hand, was a home-body. This young couple (in their mid-twenties) seemed to be devoted to one another. Quality time Edward asserted was one day out of seven.

While Edward spent most days taking messages for Kenneth, he never thought "Kenneth's getting an awful lot of calls. I wonder if he is cheating on me." Rapping this up, Kenneth was cheating. Every time he said he was going to bowl, yes he was going to bowl. But, that was just part of it. Kenneth was meeting Vaughn at the bowling alley. Vaughn, his new love interest. He wrote love letters to Vaughn and Edward found one that started out "My beloved, I cannot leave Edward but I worry that you are so weak and Edward is so strong..." Edward put the letter down. Edward finding this letter revealed Kenneth's unfaithfulness. This made their relationship a lie.

Edward played what he read of the letter over and over in his head. "Kenneth never referred to him as *my beloved*." Will Kenneth's real beloved stand up? Was Edward to believe that since they were both young that infidelity comes with the territory, expect it–ignore it?

Edward took the plunge and left Kenneth. Wherever the lies would lay, Edward refused to live a lie. If Kenneth would deny the letter, deny the man in the letter, or/and vow to be faithful, Edward knew the betrayal would hang over the relationship that he would not be able to handle or make go away.

Edward simply wanted to live a happy uncomplicated life, much like all of us. At the start of making life choices, he has realized that relationships have to be nurtured. While smothering life partners is not a good solution, giving them too much freedom unaccountable rope surely is not the best way—we search for answers. We need answers to acquiring a happy, productive, rewarding life and relationships. Let's start with a good cut of meat (easy to tenderize). Therefore why not start with a healthy slice of honesty (without any lies on the side).

I trust that we want to live happy and rewarding lives. While Kenneth and Edward vowed to be monogamous, Kenneth's infidelity broke the promise and Edward would never be the same. His security was shaken.

In order to build good, sound, healthy relationships, you must avoid the lies that are not beneficial to you or the other person. For a short period of time, the lie may stand but it cannot be preserved because of all the relating factors. When you lie and the purpose is immediate satisfaction with you consideration for the affect it will have on another, the outcome is never positive.

I kept it simple so that you could enjoy and not feel brow beaten by the vocabulary of lies.

Summary

I wrote this book to honor my mother, Alice Haywood. My entire life she has encouraged and supported me in all things and all ways—mentally, emotionally, physically, and financially. She has always tells me I am a genius. I believe it is like shooting for the moon and landing somewhere a,ong the stars. Nonetheless, it propelled me.

This book will be the turning point to uplift my mother's spirits again. Also, this book is dedicated to all my beloeved family and friends who have gone on before me, with special consideration to my grandmother, Deaconess Mamie Brown, granny. Granny was the first person who impressed upon me the importance of telling the truth and the consequences of telling a lie. My grandmother told me "If you choose to lie, that is your choice. Just remember, if you tell one lie you will have to tell another and another."

Granny also said, you must have a good memory if you want to lie. She said one thing about a lie is that it is hard to remember what you said when you lied and should that situation present itself again, you most likely will say something else, thus getting caught in that lie.

My grandmother also revealed to me that I talked in my sleep so don't lie. I was just nine when she told me these things. No way did I appreciate or understand that this information would afford me the best sleep imaginable.

I have bought into the fact that if I lied then that person made me lie, someway or another, since it was not my intention. So imagining, that someone could have that much power over me was alarming. It was as if someone could come in and steal my joy or my calm.

> Peace and quiet, meditation, no stress, drama free environments, when I have control. Yes the beginning, during, and end result is happiness. Gravitating only to things that provide comfort is the way away from lying.

It works for me. I thank my grandmother for teaching me to become a good listener. Effective communication cannot occur if the listener is speaking while the speaker is speaking or just not listening—either way the message is lost. I certainly could have easily written this book 40 years ago and shown my grandmother the dignified woman I was then at 25, but I was in a troubled marriage then and would not make that sacrifice. I regret that I did not make that stretch then although I am loving the fact that I am doing it now.

I do not believe in better late than never. There is a time for everything. And, while I am at issue with lying, I have written that sometimes you may have to lie to save your life or someone else's life. I believe that writing this book now is right time. Forgive yourself and others when lying occurs, the sooner, the better.

Seriously Yours,
Diann Banks

Message from the Author:

Hello, I am Diann Banks, at 65, relents to "it is never too late." I adopted this philosophy after reading two books by Dr. Doris A.M. Thomas, author, actress, and cancer survivor. Dr. Thomas not only lives her life to the fullest, overcoming many life threatening obstacles but she volunteers and encourages other senior citizens. Dr. Thomas has a radio show and still dances with the DC Steppers. Now 89, Dr. Thomas just stopped teaching yoga, only because time does not allow with her busy schedule. Dr. Thomas' influence sparked my desire to begin a fresh start to renew her life.

In 2011 the Office of Aging, Family Matters, Model Cities and the Cameo Club held Ms. Senior District of Columbia Pageant, where I was awarded Ms. Congeniality. I am an ambassador for the Office on Aging. March 21, 2013, I married Raymond Banks (57), a serious man of God who also calls me "a cougar" as well as "a virtuous woman".

"A woman of integrity" is how Kathy Warehime, former Human Resources manager described me in a letter of recommendation for an apartment. How can I ever forget what my manager wrote about me? Reading it changed my attitude about her as well as my work ethics. From that moment on, I did above and beyond in everything.

In addition to numerous outstanding performance awards all excelling in interpersonal skills and team building, I have been commissioned to write a book on "Manners" by a former principal of a District of Columbia Public Middle School. That book will be coming out shortly. I will give solutions to "bullying" a rapidly growing nationwide problem.

Appendix I: "Exclamations"

"You're A True Blue Girl" Former DC Councilman James Smith

"Ma, you ain't never lied." Crystal Gray

"You ain't nothing but the truth." Pamela Brinson

"You Lying" Cheryl Patterson

"We call them open-faced lies." Gladys Blount

"Everything good is not always right but everything right is always good." Regina P. Richmond

"Girl, you are always the same. You haven't changed. Everybody knows that you are good." Deborah Walsh

"People have been lying throughout generations. That is what they believe." Thomas Gray

"Some people lie about any and everything." Vanessa Williams

"I don't believe that." Thomasina Allen

Appendix II: - Short Stories:

Regina's Box 51

Run Tell That 53

Time Always Tells On Liars 66

I Am Pretty And Smart 68

Play Along Or Leave 74

Is Lying the Better Policy? 79

You Mean It 82

Don't Leave Me Out 84

Could Not Resist The Lie 92

Appendix III: Contributors

Raymond Banks

Alice Haywood

Regina P. Richmond

Dr. Seyala

Dr. Mildred P. I. Jones

Dr. Doris A.M. Thomas

Dr. Louise Dixon

Marion Williams

Thomasina Allen

Ethel and Clements Goodwine

Joann and Andrew Grady

Janice and Garland Trent

Esther Williams and Dave Yarborough

Patrick Sheehan

Christopher L. Neal

Lawrence Garr

Vince Rezendes

Roger Ferguson

Contributors = positive people who made a difference in my life.

Appendix IV: Photos and Tidbits

For your amusement as well as to support some portions of this book, I have added photos and tidbits. FYI, I am a professionally trained clown for children as well as senior citizens. No picture added to prove it. You could always book me for a show.

diannbanks948@gmail.com

Tidbit:

Four graduation pictures. Two still pictures and two action pictures. You can be sure that two are true.

My mother's graduation from Senior High School in the forty's.

Diann Bank's two graduation from College in the 90's.

Torri Eley's graduation from Senior High School 2014.

Torri

Tidbit:

One word that strike me as a lie is f**un**eral. ---- The first three letters are misleading for me. I always wanted to have a funeral like the one I described in my 11th grade English paper. One day I was watching television and I saw my story with a twist.

My paper was about how many people come out to your funeral but won't come out to support you in anything in life. I wrote that I would be on death's bed but not dead and I would hear everything that someone would say at my casket or to me.. Depending on the intensity of the statement, I would rise up and scare them to death. My teacher said that was an interesting way to look at death. I was 16 and cognizant then about real and fake people. (The truth versus the lie.)

The name of the paper?? This Should Be FUN. I did get an "A."

Tidbit:

Another Poem

Yes I am admitting that I lie
And you know I'll never say if I'm lying I'm flying.
And you are sitting there wondering why
I lie for several reasons And we have several seasons
I won't run out of lies, that just can't be
So, I lie and lie and let it be.

poem

My little sister, Big G. The only thing big about my sister is her heart.

Tidbit:

It's written all over your face. (That you are telling a lie.)

Face of three birthday cakes.

1. Happy Birthday Diann Queen For A Day
2. I Corinthians 13:11
3. Psalms 27:14

Tidbit:

The man who appears homeless says "I want some change to get a drink." He is being honest, I give him some change. The next woman he asked preached to him about wanting a drink. I asked her how she felt about him being honest. She told me I was right, preached a little more to the man, but gave him a dollar. If he had lied to me, I would not have given him anything.

Tidbit:

I don't believe it. What?—these are the responses you get when you tell somebody something about another person and they cannot conceive or believe it because it is so unlike the character of that person.

I

Tidbit:

I found my best picture of myself (with a nearly bald head) and my favorite picture of an Indian girl with hair flowing to the ground and merged them. The Indian girl looked so much like me that I had to take her picture out, put my picture in place of her picture, and compare the pictures. All four pictures are different yet I have said on numerous occasions that they are all me. It is the truth to me but the truth is only three of the pictures are me.

Tidbit:

A popular, famous (maybe most used) lie is.......... "IT'S
IN
THE
MAIL."

Tidbit:

IT'S FREE. YOU ONLY HAVE TO PAY SHIPPING
AND HANDLING.

Tidbit:

All tied up not really tied up literally.

Tidbit:

Lipstick on your collar - tell, tell- sign

Tidbit:

Proof - tape recording, signature, authentic document, valid data, logical facts, photos, the real thing, science. All in all. It boils down to belief.

Tidbit:

Fantasy, fiction, fairy tale, myth, legend, urban legend, old wise tale, fabrication. Again, truth or lie is in the mind of the beholder's belief.

Tidbit:

Half a truth is often a great lie. B. Franklin

Tidbit:

You can fool some of the people some of the time, but you can't fool all of the people all of the time.

Tidbit:

Just poking fun, just fooling. (When an adverse reaction is a result of a lie.)

Tidbit:

True and false tests may be perceived as easy tests. In reality, these tests are the most difficult because one unaware or looked over word change will change the answer.

Tidbit:

Stretching the truth? A lie.